Jus' Sharn' Tidbits

Volume 1 Devotions

JUS' SHARN' TIDBITS

Volume 1 Devotions

LadyG

XULON PRESS

Xulon Press
555 Winderley Pl, Suite 225
Maitland, FL 32751
407.339.4217
www.xulonpress.com

© 2024 by LadyG

All rights reserved solely by the author. The author guarantees all contents are original and do not infringe upon the legal rights of any other person or work. No part of this book may be reproduced in any form without the permission of the author.

Due to the changing nature of the Internet, if there are any web addresses, links, or URLs included in this manuscript, these may have been altered and may no longer be accessible. The views and opinions shared in this book belong solely to the author and do not necessarily reflect those of the publisher. The publisher therefore disclaims responsibility for the views or opinions expressed within the work.

Unless otherwise indicated, Scripture quotations taken from the New King James Version (NKJV). Copyright © 1982 by Thomas Nelson, Inc. Used by permission. All rights reserved.

Paperback ISBN-13: 979-8-86850-606-2
Ebook ISBN-13: 979-8-86850-607-9

DEDICATION

My dedication to God, my Heavenly Father, who never gave up on me, for God knows what we need in time, this is the time for Jus' Sharn' Tibits, God planted this seed within me, and the watering of the seed began with hearing His Words through scripture, through a message, whether through a book and or through music.

To my parents Chester and Lula Irene with whom instilled Christian values in my upbringing.

I pray that Jus' Sharn' will be encouraging to you as it has been for me to share these devotions with you.

What a journey a long time coming with this, this has been a self-confidence builder and for me to understand and receive who God says, "I am". Thank you, my Heavenly Father.

> **2 Timothy 2v15** - *Be diligent to present yourself approved to God, a worker who does not need to be ashamed, rightly dividing the word of truth.*

THANK YOU

I specifically and gratefully want to Thank Evangelist Katherine Leonard and her Husband Brother Alvin Leonard for sharing Jus' Sharn' Tidbits on their Radio Internet Broadcast Christian Ministry "Let's Talk About It", since 2019 and still being presented, All Glory To God!

To my Loving Husband Duran, thank you for encouraging and a reminder to complete volume 1 of Jus' Sharn' Tidbits.

Thanks to everyone on my publishing team for your patience and helping me get through.

God Bless To All…

—TABLE OF TIDBITS—

Introduction xi
#1–Let's Do a Checklist 1
#2–Staying Connected 3
#3–A New Normal 5
#4–He is Great 7
#5–God's Love 9
#6–Crossroads 10
#7–Believe 12
#8–Detox 13
#9–Joy 15
#10–Anchor 16
#11–Waymaker 18
#12–Rise Up 20
#13–Wonderfully Made 24
#14–I Cannot Breathe 26

#15–Blessed 28

#16–Blesses to Blessings 31

#17–Just Sharing a Reminder 34

#18–Listening 37

#19–Armor of God 39

#20–Royalty 41

#21–Guilt 43

#22–Acknowledgement to God 45

#23–There is Power in the Name of Jesus Christ.... 47

#24–Give Thanks 50

#25–God Will Keep You 53

#26–A Time to Celebrate in the Month of December (Life) – Part I. 55

#27 – A Time to Celebrate in the Month of December (Life) – Part II 58

#28 – A Time to Celebrate in the Month of December (Life) – Part III 60

#29–Reflection of the Year 2020 63

Conclusion 65

Just Me 67

—INTRODUCTION—

The purpose behind our Jus' Sharn' Tidbits is to offer encouragement that will speak to your spirit, soul, mind, and body. The tidbits gathered within this first volume came from the crazy year of 2020, when the COVID-19 pandemic was in full swing, the presidential election was underway, and so much more.

Praise be to God that we made it through that year. Now, we wish to share with you our words of encouragement and inspiration for you to take with you no matter where you go.

Be encouraged.
Peace and Blessings.

> *"As iron sharpens iron, so a man sharpens the countenance of his friend."* **Proverbs 27:17 (NKJV)**

Jus' Sharn' a Tidbit—#1
—LET'S DO A CHECKLIST—

- Can you hear sounds? Yes, you can hear.

- Can you see colors, lights, day, and night? Yes, you can see.

- Can you smell a vast array of aromas? Yes, you can smell. Breathe in the fresh air.

- Can you enjoy the taste of crisp cool refreshing water? Yes, you can taste.

- Can you touch? Yes, you can touch and feel.

These five basic senses are to remind you how blessed we are and that no matter what challenges we face, we have the goodness of God to be thankful for. Raise your hands and give thanks.

> *"O taste and see that the LORD is good: blessed is the man who trusts in Him."* **Psalm 34:8 (NKJV)**

Embrace God's blessings, goodness, and love. Peace and Blessings.

Jus' Sharn' a Tidbit – #2
—STAYING CONNECTED—

We are in a time of how we can reflect upon ourselves, mind, body, soul, and spirit. We have witnessed and experienced much through this time of uncertainty. My question to you is what changes have you made during this time?

Remember, we have a God who will see us through any unfavorable challenge. I encourage you to stay focused and stay connected.

> *"Pray without ceasing."* **1 Thessalonians 5:17 (NKJV)**

> *"Keep yourselves in the love of God, for the mercy of our Lord Jesus Christ unto eternal life."* **Jude 1:21 (NKJV)**

Peace and Blessings.

Song of the Day: "Be Connected" by Rev. Jackie McCullough

Jus' Sharn' a Tidbit – #3
—A NEW NORMAL—

In the past months, we have lived through a pandemic where we had to make some important decisions. Whether they were favorable or not, we had to make changes in our lives. For those who may feel it was a disruption of everyday life, remember this: nothing stays the same. Seasons come and seasons go. We had to embrace of living a "new normal." Embrace the change for God is still in control. Be encouraged.

> *"To everything there is a season, and a time to every purpose under the heaven: A time to be born, and a time to die; a time to plant, and a time to pluck up that which is planted. A time to kill, and a time to heal; a time to break down, and a time to build up. A time to weep, and a time to laugh; a time to mourn, and a time to dance. A time to cast away stones, and a time to gather stones together; a time to embrace, and a time to refrain from embracing. A time to get,*

and a time to lose; a time to keep, and a time to cast away. A time to rend, and a time to sew; a time to keep silence, and a time to speak. A time to love, and a time to hate, a time of war, and a time of peace. What profit hath he that worketh in that wherein he laboureth? I have seen the travail, which God hath given to the sons of men to be exercised in it. He hath made everything beautiful in his time: also, he hath set the world in their heart, so that no man can find out the work that God maketh from the beginning to the end. I know that there is no good in them, but for a man to rejoice, and to do good in his life. And, that every man should eat and drink, and enjoy the good of all his labour, it is the gift of God. I know that whatsoever God doeth, it shall be forever: nothing can be put to it, nor any thing taken from it: and God doeth it, that men should fear before him. That which hath is now; and that which is to be hath already been and God requireth that which is past." **Ecclesiastes 3:1-15 (NKJV)**

Look up, smile, and live. Give God praise.
Peace and Blessings.

Song of the Day: "Hold On (Changed Is Comin" by Sounds of Blackness

Jus' Sharn' a Tidbit – #4
—HE IS GREAT—

"Bless the Lord, O my soul! O Lord my God, you are very great! You are clothed with splendor and majesty." **Psalm 104:1 (NKJV)**

Let all the Earth rejoice! Just want you to be encouraged and remind you of how good God is. We cannot praise Him enough!

My tidbit for today is giving reference to God. Yes, we have encountered some life-changing occurrences, yet we still give Him praise and honor. Glory to God!

I want you to reflect on where you are right now. If you need to make a change, make it. It is up to you to make that choice.

I will leave these verses with you:

"Great is our Lord and mighty in power; His understanding is infinite." **Psalm 147:5 (NKJV)**

> *"Let the heavens rejoice, and let the earth be glad, and let them say among the nations, "the Lord reigns."* **1 Chronicles 16:31 (NKJV)**

Peace and Blessings.

Song of the Day: "How Great Is Our God" by Hezekiah Walker

Jus' Sharn' a Tidbit – #5
—GOD'S LOVE—

God loves you. Do you believe that? Do you feel the love of God? God waits for you to have a relationship with Him.

Love is patient and love is kind.

Repeat this to yourself daily. He shows real love when we feel we do not deserve it, but we do. God is love. His love is patient, and His love is kind and sweet. Seek Him. You will start experiencing and understanding the love of God. Find the love of God.

> *"For God so loved the world that He gave his one and only Son, that whoever believes in him shall not perish but have eternal life."*
> **John 3:16 (NKJV)**

Peace and Blessings.

Song of the Day: "No Greater Love" by Smokie Norful

Jus' Sharn' a Tidbit — #6
—CROSSROADS—

There comes a time in our lives when we may have thoughts of our past and thoughts of our future. Your thoughts may have you really look at yourself and ask questions like:

What am I doing?

- Where am I going?

- What does my future entail?

It does not matter what age you are. Just ask yourself, "Am I yea or nay?" In other words, are you in the middle of which path to take for your relationship with God, yea or nay?

I want to conform to God's ways as I continue to live. Do not allow the inner you to be your enemy. You must decide what matters to you when you find yourself at a crossroad. Yea or nay?

Please read and reflect on the following Scriptures: (NKJV)

- Jeremiah 6:16

- Matthew 7:13-14

- 1 Peter 5:8

- Romans 3:23

- 2 Timothy 2:15

God bless and keep moving forward.
Peace and Blessings.

Song of the Day: "He's Able" by Deitrick Haddon

Jus' Sharn' a Tidbit – #7
—BELIEVE—

"He who believes in ME, as the scripture has said, out of his heart will flow rivers of living waters." **John 7:38 : (NKJV)**

Believe. Believe.

This is being shared with you not only as a reminder, but to share with others who do not believe. It is about you. God speaks to us within. Are you listening? Believe in Him.

Peace and Blessings.

Song of the Day: "I Believe" by Marvin Sapp

Jus' Sharn' a Tidbit – #8
—DETOX—

Please take heed of the word of God. This is the time to look within yourself and strengthen your relationship with God.

> *"Let us draw near with a true heart in full assurance of faith, having our hearts sprinkle from an evil conscience and our bodies washed with pure water."* **Hebrews 10:22 (NKJV)**

Detox is a process or period of time in which one abstains or rids the body, mind, soul, and spirit from unhealthy substances, not only food, drink, and drugs.

What are you feeding your spirit? What do you need to detox from? Is it pain, uncertainty, loneliness, unhappiness, unforgiveness, negativity, jealousy, envy, fear, just to name a few? Let your heart be massaged with the holy words from God **(Ephesians 5:26)**, that He might sanctify and cleanse it with the washing of water by the word.

Detoxing yourself within will bring you peace, joy, and happiness. It will rebuild, renew, and restore not only with your relationship with God, but will also bring clarity of your purpose.

> *"Then I sprinkle clean water on you, and you will be clean, I will cleanse you from all filthiness and from all your idols."* **Ezekiel 36:25 (NKJV)**

God bless and keep moving forward.
Peace and Blessings.

Song of the Day: "Create In Me a Clean Heart" by Donnie McClurkin

Jus' Sharn' a Tidbit – #9
— JOY —

Do you still have joy? We are in the times of living in a chaotic world. When listening to the media and hearing all that is going on in times like these, do you still have joy? Feeling hopelessness? Do not.

In the Book of Nehemiah, chapter eight tells us how God reminded the people of how He works to rebuild, renew, and restore. Now is the time for repentance and deliverance.

> *"Then he said to them, "Go your way, eat the fat, drink the sweet, and send portions to those for whom nothing is prepared; for this day is holy to our Lord. Do not sorrow, for the joy of the Lord is your strength."* **Nehemiah 8:10 (NKJV)**

Be encouraged.
Peace and Blessings.

Song of the Day: "Count It All Joy" by The Winans

Jus' Sharn' a Tidbit – #10
—ANCHOR—

Is your mind, body, and soul anchored in the Lord?

> *"You will keep Him in perfect peace whose mind is stayed on You, because he trusts in You."* **Isaiah 26:3 (NKJV)**

> *"Wisdom and knowledge will be the stability of your times, and the strength of salvation, the fear of the Lord is His treasure."* **Isaiah 33:6 (NKJV)**

> *"He will not be afraid of evil things; His heart is steadfast, trusting in the Lord."* **Psalm 112:7 (NKJV)**

"My soul, wait silently for God alone, for my expectation is from Him." **Psalm 62:5 (NKJV)**

Peace and blessings.

Jus' Sharn' a Tidbit – #11
—WAYMAKER—

We go through life with either seeing eyes or blinders. We think when we are thrown into situations, we will not make it. We pace the floor, bite our nails, smoke, eat, cry, and drink. In other words, we worry, but why?

We serve an all-time loving God. He does allow situations to enter our tiny worlds and we think there is no way out, but this is not true. God is a Waymaker. He allows us to live life, but ask yourself, how do you choose to live your life? He makes a way out of no way that we can see. Walk by faith and not by sight.

> *"But Jesus looked at them and said to them, 'With men this is impossible, but with God all things are possible.'"* **Matthew 19:26 (NKJV)**

God's words never fail.

> *"Behold this day I am going the way of all the earth. And you know in all your hearts and in all your souls that not one thing has failed of all the good things which the Lord your God spoke concerning you. All have come to pass for you; not one word of them has failed."*
> **Joshua 23:14 (NKJV)**

God keeps all of His promises. He is a Waymaker and a Promise Keeper.

> *"For all the promises of God in Him are Yes, and in Him Amen, to the glory of God through us."* **2 Corinthians 1:20 (NKJV)**

God is faithful.
Peace and blessings.

Song of the Day: "Way Maker" by Sinach

Jus' Sharn' a Tidbit – #12
—RISE UP—

This is not just about color of your skin. This is about you. Rise up. Embrace the hand that is outstretched to you. Embrace the love and Word of God. Strengthen your relationship with Him. Understand and know your purpose. It is not too late.

Rise up, children of God, rise up. Take back what the devil has stolen from you.

—RISE UP—

"Do not rejoice over me, my enemy; when I fall, I will arise; when I sit in darkness, the Lord will be a light to me." **Micah 7:8 (NKJV)**

—RISE UP—

"Arise, for this matter is your responsibility. We also are with you. Be of good courage and do it." **Ezra 10:4 (NKJV)**

—RISE UP—

"The Lord is my strength and my shield; my heart trusted in Him, and I am helped; therefore, my heart greatly rejoices, and with my song I will praise Him." **Psalm 28:7 (NKJV)**

—RISE UP—

"Shake yourself from the dust and arise; sit down, O Jerusalem; loose yourself from the bonds of your neck, O captive daughter of Zion." **Isaiah 52:2 (NKJV)**

—RISE UP—

"Arise, shine, for your light has come and the glory of the Lord is risen upon you. For behold darkness shall cover the earth, and deep darkness the peoples; but the Lord will arise over you and his glory will be seen upon you. The Gentiles shall come to your light, and kings to the brightness of your rising." **Isaiah 60:1-3 (NKJV)**

—RISE UP—

"For a righteous man may fall seven times and rise again, but the wicked shall fall by calamity." **Proverbs 24:16 (NKJV)**

—RISE UP—

"But rise and stand on your feet, for I have appeared to you for this purpose, to make you a minister and a witness both of the things in which you have seen and of the things which I will yet reveal to you." **Acts 26:16 (NKJV)**

—RISE UP—

"Which is easier, to say, 'Your sins are forgiven you,' or to say, 'Rise and walk?'" **Luke 5:23 (NKJV)**

—RISE UP—

"For whatever is born of God overcomes the world and this is the victory that has overcome the world-our faith." **1 John 5:4 (NKJV)**

"From the rising of the sun to its going down, the Lord's name is to be praised!" **Psalm 113:3 (NKJV)**

—RISE UP—

Peace and blessings.

Song of the Day: "Still I Rise" by Yolanda Adams

Jus' Sharn' a Tidbit – #13
—WONDERFULLY MADE—

> *"I will praise you for I am fearfully and wonderfully made. Marvelous are Your works, and that my soul knows very well."* **Psalm 139:14 (NKJV)**

I have a question for you. Does your soul know itself very well? Think about it. You look at yourself in the mirror, but what do you see? Do you feel beautifully and wonderfully made?

> *"And do not be conformed to this world, but be transformed by the renewing of your mind, that you may prove what is that good and acceptable and perfect will of God."* **Romans 12:2 (NKJV)**

Remember, God created man in His own image. What image do you portray? What impression do you portray to others as well as to yourself? We as children of God should be able to love one another and allow the Word of God to renew our minds and hearts, and present our bodies as a living sacrifice, holy and acceptable to God.

If you do not feel beautifully, fearfully, and wonderfully made, drape yourself in the Word of God. God's words are pure.

> Embrace thyself. Love you as God loves you.
> Peace and blessings.
>
> **Song of the Day:** "I Know Who I Am" by Sinach

Jus' Sharn' a Tidbit – #14
—I CANNOT BREATHE—

This is not about a knee on the neck, "I can't breathe." This is not about a COVID-19 health issue or wearing a mask, "I can't breathe." It is that feeling when you are awakened in the night with the feeling of anxiety, "I can't breathe." The having a panic attack, "I can't breathe."

My question to you is, "Why can't you breathe?"

> *"And the Lord God formed man of the dust of the ground and breathed into his nostrils the breath of life; and man became a living being."* **Genesis 2:7 (NKJV)**

We are living and breathing. Just think about this if you are having trouble breathing. Is it because of your uncertainty with your relationship with the Lord thy God? He can heal and deliver.

Let us think about Job and all that he went through. Through everything, he still had faith. *"As long as my breath is in me, and the breath of God in my nostrils."* **Job 27:3 (NKJV)**

I want to encourage you. You may have to wear a mask, or you may be suffering with an illness. The enemy may have a knee on your neck, but God will still deliver, heal, and protect you.

I leave this with you. *"Let everything that has breath praise the Lord. Praise the Lord."* **Psalm 150:6 (NKJV)**

Peace and blessings.
Song of the Day: "Breathe" by Maverick City Music

Jus' Sharn' a Tidbit – #15
—BLESSED—

What is your definition of **blessed**? What does **blessed** mean to you?

Here are a few Scriptures about being **blessed**:

> "***Blessed*** *be the God and Father of our Lord Jesus Christ, who has **blessed** us with all spiritual blessing in the heavenly places in Christ."* **Ephesians 1:3 (NKJV)**

> "***Blessed*** *are the poor in spirit, for theirs is the kingdom of heaven.* ***Blessed*** *are those who mourn, for they shall be comforted.* ***Blessed*** *are the meek, for they shall inherit the earth.* ***Blessed*** *are those who hunger and thirst for righteousness, for they shall be filled.* ***Blessed*** *are the merciful, for they shall obtain mercy.* ***Blessed*** *are the pure in heart, for they shall see God.* ***Blessed*** *are the peacemakers, for they*

shall be called sons of God. ***Blessed*** *are those who are persecuted for righteousness sake, for theirs is the kingdom of heaven.* ***Blessed*** *are you when they revile and persecute you and say all kinds of evil against you falsely for My sake."* **Matthew 5:3-12 (NKJV)**

*"**Blessed** shall you be when you come in, and **blessed** shall you be when you go out."* **Deuteronomy 28:6 (NKJV)**

*"**Blessed** is the man who trusts in the Lord. And whose hope is the Lord."* **Jeremiah 17:7 (NKJV)**

*"**Blessed** is the one who comes in the name of the Lord. We have blessed you from the house of the Lord."* **Psalm 118:26 (NKJV)**

*"**Blessed** be the name of the Lord. From this time forth and forevermore."* **Psalm 113:2 (NKJV)**

Do you feel that your life is blessed? Look at your life. Only you can make the change in your life if you feel that you need to make a change. We are blessed to be alive!

Peace and blessings.

Song of the Day: "We're Blessed" by Fred Hammond

Jus' Sharn' a Tidbit – #16
—BLESSES TO BLESSINGS—

There is a difference between the words "bless" and "blessings." To "bless" is to take action to bless others while a "blessing" is a gift given by God.

Enjoy the blessings of peace like a short prayer of thanks before a meal or the act of praying for divine protection.

Blesses to blessings from one to another. God blesses us with His blessings. All blessings come from God. Just think about how God blesses us each day. How God sacrificed His only Son for us. How does His Word bless us? It educates our consciences of how to live, how to see this world, and how to maintain through our tribulations. God blesses our lives.

Ask yourself this, "How do you bless God in return?" God's Word blesses each individual. Does the Word of

God cause you to pray and praise Him? What about God's blessings for your life?

> *"Commit your works to the Lord, and your thoughts will be established."* **Proverbs 16:3 (NKJV)**

> *"The blessing of the Lord, it makes one rich, and he adds no sorrow with it."* **Proverbs 10:22 (NKJV)**

> *"I will make them and the places all around My hill a blessing and I will cause the showers to come down in their season; there shall be showers of blessing."* **Ezekiel 34:26 (NKJV)**

God has given us everything. His blessings are amazing.

Read **1 Samuel 25:6** for a simple blessing prayer. To receive God's blessings, look within. Are you ready to deal within yourself? Cleanse your mind, clean up your act, and know God for yourself. You will not regret it.

Bless to blessed to blesses to blessings. These are the teachings of the Word of God for us to grow. To live by His Word and be a blessing to someone else. It could be financial blessings, a hug, or a smile, or just some help to someone.

You may never know where a blessing can come from. My life has been and continues to be a blessing from God. Hallelujah!

Every day is a **blessing** from God.

I leave this simple prayer with you:

> *My Heavenly Father, I humbly come to You. God, please continue to bless us, to guide us, to keep us safe, to show us how to give love, how to live a peaceful healthy life as we continue to shower you in prayer, worship, and praise. Thank you, God. In Jesus's name, we pray. Amen.*

Song of the Day: "Blessings on Blessings" by Anthony Brown

Jus' Sharn' a Tidbit – #17
—JUST SHARING A REMINDER—

We are coming upon the holiday seasons. Let us think back to the past months full of COVID, sickness, presidential elections, rioting, black lives matter, a dive in finances in businesses and households, and even death. Now we find ourselves in flu/COVID season.

How do you feel? Do you feel fear and uncertainty? Are you questioning to yourself, "What is God doing?" Has He heard the prayers from His people?

> *"If my people, who are called by My name, will humble themselves and pray, seek My face and turn from their wicked ways; then will I hear from heaven and will forgive their sin, and will heal their land."* **2 Chronicles 7:14 (NKJV)**

Now in this month of October and the coming months to the end of the year, my question to you is, "How do you feel and where are your thoughts?"

This is the time of season the enemy becomes very busy as he tries to overwhelm our minds with stress, worry, anxiety, depression, loneliness, and even suicidal thoughts.

This is not the time to fall into the thoughts of what the enemy is planting in your mind.

This is the time to give thanks to God, not to wait for Thanksgiving or Christmas, but right now. Wherever you are, give thanks for waking up, breathing, seeing, hearing, smelling, tasting, and smiling. Give a fist bump of acknowledgment (due to the six feet social distancing protocol) to someone or give a hug. Just tell someone that you care that you love them, and that God loves them, too. This is the time to acknowledge God in all of His ways. Show kindness, give a meal to someone, and do not allow the enemy to come into your home. Fill it with thanksgiving and love.

These Scriptures I leave with you. Jus' Sharn' some reminders.

> *"In everything give thanks, for this is the will of God in Christ Jesus for you."*
> **1 Thessalonians 5:18 (NKJV)**

> *"Giving thanks always for all things to God the Father in the name of our Lord Jesus Christ."* **Ephesians 5:20 (NKJV)**

> *"Bless the Lord, O my Soul, and forget not all His benefits."* **Psalm 103:2 (NKJV)**

> *"Enter into His gates with thanksgiving and His courts with praise. Give thanks to Him; and bless His name!"* **Psalm 100:4 (NKJV)**

> *"Oh, give thanks to the God of heaven, for His mercy endures forever."* **Psalm 136:26 (NKJV)**

I cannot thank Him enough. We have so much to be thankful. Amen.

Song of the Day: "Thank You Jesus" by Brent Jones

Jus' Sharn' a Tidbit – #18
—LISTENING—

"So, then, my beloved brethren, let every man be swift to hear, slow to speak, slow to wrath."
James 1:19 (NKJV)

Are you listening to what God is saying? Do you hear His voice? What is He telling you right now?

We are in chaotic situations what with dealing with COVID-19, flu season, racial discrimination, voting, financial situations, healthcare, and homelessness to name a few. When you look within yourself, it all seems hopeless, but you cannot allow fear to lock you in. Are we not listening to the voice of God?

His Word is His voice. We see with our eyes, but do we see with our faith? Are we listening to what God is saying? The world is so out of control, but I am asking you, are you listening? Are you paying attention to what God is saying to the world? The enemy is trying to keep us off focus. Children of God, humble yourselves and pray. Unite in prayer.

> *"But He said, 'More than that, Blessed are those who hear the word of God and keep it!'"* **Luke 11:28 (NKJV)**

> *"The things which you learned and received and heard and saw in me, these do, and the God of peace will be with you."* **Philippians 4:9 (NKJV)**

Song of the Day: "Listen" by Marvin Sapp

Jus' Sharn' a Tidbit — #19
— ARMOR OF GOD —

The breast plate of armor. God speaks.

> *"Finally, my brethren, be strong in the Lord and in the power of His might. Put on the whole armor of God, that you may be able to stand against the wiles of the devil. For we do not wrestle against flesh and blood, but against principalities, against powers, against the rulers of the darkness of this age, against spiritual hosts of wickedness in the heavenly places. Therefore, take up the whole armor of God, that you may be able to withstand in the evil day, and having done all, to stand. Stand therefore, having girded your waist with truth, having put on the breastplate of righteousness, and having shod your feet with the preparation of the gospel of peace, above all, taking the shield of faith with which, you*

> *will be able to quench all the fiery darts of the wicked one. And take the helmet of salvation, and the sword of the Spirit, which is the word of God."* **Ephesians 6:10-17 (NKJV)**

Jus' Sharn' that this verse simply says arm yourself with your armor of God's Word and pray.

Peace and blessings.

Song of the Day: "Armor of God" by Shirley Caesar

Jus' Sharn' a Tidbit – #20
— ROYALTY —

Do you know whose you are and whom you are? You are purpose for God. You are royalty, you are made in His image.

> *"Do you know that you are God's temple and that God's Spirit dwells in you?"* **1 Corinthians 3:16 (NKJV)**

> *"You shall also be a crown of glory in the hand of the Lord and a royal diadem in hand of your God."* **Isaiah 62:3 (NKJV)**

> *"But you are a chosen generation, a Royal Priest hood, a Holy Nation, His own special people, that you may proclaim the praises of Him who called you out of darkness into His marvelous light."* **1 Peter 2:9 (NKJV)**

Know who you are and whose you are. Fear not.
"For the kingdom is the Lord's, and He rules over the nations." **Psalm 22:28 (NKJV)**

> *"As obedient children, not conforming yourselves to the former lusts, as in your ignorance; but as He who called you is holy, you also be holy in all your conduct, because it is written; "Be holy, for I am holy."'* **1 Peter 1:14-16 (NKJV)**

> *"Therefore, if anyone is in Christ, he is a new creation; old things have passed away; behold, all things have become new."* **2 Corinthians 5:17 (NKJV)**

> *"For you are a holy people to the Lord your God; the Lord your God has chosen you to be a people for Himself, a special treasure above all the peoples on the face of the earth."* **Deuteronomy 7:6 (NKJV)**

Hold your head up, look up to the heavens, and smile. Know you are royalty. Be encouraged.

Peace and blessings.

Song of the Day: "Royalty" by Tasha Cobbs

Jus' Sharn' a Tidbit – #21
—GUILT—

Are you struggling with guilt? Guilty of not forgiving yourself or someone else? How do you deal with your guilt? Do you suppress and/or deny your guilt? How much guilt are you carrying?

The devil attacks our thoughts with guilt; thus, we feel guilty because we fall short because we have sinned against God. God sacrificed His only begotten Son for our transgressions. You can be set free if you only believe.

Guilt has a negative impact on your mental health, but God's Word can erase and cleanse.

> *"Little children, let no man deceive you: he who practices righteousness is righteous, just as He is righteous."* **1 John 3:7 (NKJV)**

> *"Now by this we know that we know Him if we keep His commandments. He who says, "I know Him," and does not keep His*

> *commandments, is a liar, and the truth is not in him."* **1 John 2:3-4 (NKJV)**
>
> *"Let us draw near with a true heart in full assurance of faith, having our hearts sprinkled from an evil conscience and our bodies washed with pure water."* **Hebrews 10:22 (NKJV)**

Believe His Word and cleansed thyself.
Peace and blessings.

Song of the Day: "Break Every Chain" by Tasha Cobbs

Jus' Sharn' a Tidbit – #22
—ACKNOWLEDGEMENT TO GOD—

"O Lord, You are the portion of my inheritance and my cup; You maintain my lot. The lines have fallen to me in pleasant places; Yes, I have a good inheritance. I will bless the Lord, who has given me counsel; my heart also instructs me in the night seasons. I have set the Lord always before me; because He is at my right hand, I shall not be moved. Therefore, my heart is glad, and my glory rejoices: my flesh also shall rest in hope."
Psalms 16:5-9 (NKJV)

Children of God let us give thanks to our Lord thy God. He has blessed us so much during this season and past seasons. November is the month of Thanksgiving and giving thanks. My question for you is, "Are you giving

Him thanks on a daily basis and acknowledging His blessings for grace and mercy?"

Let us not wait for the Thanksgiving season, for Thanksgiving is every day as we are awakening every morning by Him. He orders our steps as He protects, comforts us, and fulfills our needs. Give yourself to Him as He has given us Him.

Believe His Word and be encouraged.

Peace and blessings.

Song of the Day: "Give Me You" by Shana Wilson

Jus' Sharn' a Tidbit – #23
—THERE IS POWER IN THE NAME OF JESUS CHRIST—

> *"Nor there is salvation in any other, for there is no other name under heaven given among men by which we must be saved."* **Acts 4:12 (NKJV)**

We know about salvation but remember that salvation comes from no one else but in the name of Jesus Christ. God sacrificed His begotten Son, Jesus. Why? For us. Here is your proof.

> *"For no other foundation can anyone lay than that which is laid, which is Jesus Christ."* **1 Corinthians 3:11 (NKJV)**

> *"And this is the testimony, that God has given us eternal life and this life is in His Son. He*

> *who has the Son has life: he who does not have the Son of God does not have life."* **1 John 5:11-12 (NKJV)**

Now, is the time to get your house in order. We still have a chance. Do not procrastinate for we are in out last days. Let us get it together. We grieve and worry over others, but remember this, we are born and taken from our mother's womb alone; therefore, we stand before God alone. We intercede for others but let our light shine before others where we are the example. Living for Christ brings peace, love, and happiness. We cast our burdens before Him. We belong to Jesus Christ.

There is power in the name of Jesus for repentance, deliverance, healing, grief, brokenness, and forgiveness. For every knee shall bow and every tongue shall confess Jesus is Lord. Just call the name of Jesus.

Believe His Word and be encouraged.

Peace and blessings.

Song of the Day: "Something About the Name of Jesus" by Rance Allen and Kirk Franklin

In loving memory of Rance Allen "I Stood on the Banks of Jordan."

> *"Blessed are those who mourn, for they shall be comforted."* **Matthew 5:4 (NKJV)**

Write your thoughts.

Jus' Sharn' a Tidbit – #24
—GIVE THANKS—

There are many Scriptures for give thanks! Even though this is Thanksgiving week, let us give thanks to our Lord and Savior Jesus Christ!

Just think, where would you be today if it were not for Him? We should give thanks daily. Acknowledge Him as you open your eyes to begin your day.

> *"Oh, give thanks to the God of heaven! For His mercy endures forever."* **Psalm 136:26 (NKJV)**

> *"Thanks be to God for His indescribable gift!"* **2 Corinthians 9:15 (NKJV)**

> *"Now therefore, our God, we thank You and praise Your glorious name."* **1 Chronicles 29:13 (NKJV)**

> *"Sing praise to the Lord, you saints of His, and give thanks at the remembrance of His holy name."* **Psalm 30:4 (NKJV)**

> *"I will praise the name of the God with a song and will magnify Him with thanksgiving."* **Psalm 69:30 (NKJV)**

My prayer of Thanksgiving.

> *Lord God, I thank you. I thank you for every blessing You have bestowed upon me and upon my family and friends. My prayer that everyone worldwide will bow to You in worship, with praise to give thanks for the blessings of keeping us day by day, not only to celebrate Thanksgiving, but to let You know how grateful we are for keeping us this day. I pray we all can unite in harmony to worship and praise You, Lord. I pray that we can forgive and show that all is forgiven as You do for us daily. I am so grateful. Gratefulness is flowing from my heart to have this opportunity to say, thank you, God, My Lord, and Savior Jesus Christ. Amen.*

Jus' Sharn' thanks you for reading our tidbits! Believe His Word and be encouraged.

Peace and blessings.

Song of the Day: "You Are Good" by Israel Houghton

Jus' Sharn' a Tidbit – #25
—GOD WILL KEEP YOU—

To be kept by God! Hallelujah!

> *"You are my hiding place; you shall preserve me from trouble; you shall surround me with songs of deliverance. Selah."* **Psalm 32:7 (NKJV)**

Do not get discouraged, keep fasting and praying. He is able to protect, comfort, and strengthen. He is a Burden Carrier and a Keeper. I can truly say of each word that was spoken; He has done it for me. I tried Him. Will you try Him, too? Allow Him to keep you for the peace that He will give you, oh, my, my! To be kept by God!

> *"To an inheritance, incorruptible and undefiled and that does not fade away, reserved in heaven for you, who are kept by the power of God through faith for salvation ready*

to be revealed in the last time." **1 Peter 1:4-5 (NKJV)**

To be kept by the only most high God. I have made some unhealthy decisions, but God was my security blanket during that season. To be kept by God. When I wanted to give up, God kept me. During the crying sleepless nights, God has kept me. To be kept by God.

I encourage you not to give up and not to let go of God. God is a Keeper through whatever life brings your way.

Believe His Word and be encouraged.

Peace and blessings.

Song of the Day: "He Kept Me" by Kurt Carr

Jus' Sharn' a Tidbit — #26
—A TIME TO CELEBRATE IN THE MONTH OF DECEMBER (LIFE)—

(Part I)

Exhale! We are in December, the last month, and it is time to take a moment to reflect on the last year.

COVID-19,

- Homelessness
- Grief
- Pain
- Election

- Black lives matter

- Finances

- Changes in your lifestyle

- Other circumstances

It all seems a little grim but think about this. If you are reading this tidbit, you are alive. Praise God! Even though it may have seemed so unpleasant this year, just remember that we will be celebrating Jesus for this is the month to celebrate His birth. What an amazing gift to be bestowed upon us!

Let us take the time to show compassion, love, kindness, and patience, but we all know the greatest of these is the love of God. Look at yourself and embrace yourself. Love on yourself because you are wonderfully made in His sight and always remember that you are so loved by God.

> *"Men shall utter the memory of Your great goodness and shall sing of Your righteousness. They shall abundantly utter the memory of thy great goodness and shall sing of thy righteousness. The Lord is gracious and full of compassion; slow to anger, and of great mercy. The Lord is good to all: and his tender*

mercies are over all his works." **Psalms 145:6-9 (NKJV)**

"I will mention the lovingkindness of the Lord, and the praises of the Lord, according to all that the Lord hath bestowed on us and the great goodness toward the house of Israel, which he hath bestowed on them according to his mercies and according to the multitude of his lovingkindness." **Isaiah 63:7 (NKJV)**

"And also, that every man should eat and drink and enjoy the good of all his labor, it is the gift of God." **Ecclesiastes 3:13(NKJV)**

Celebrate you and your family and be encouraged. Peace and blessings.

Song of the Day: "Let's Celebrate" by Stephen Hurd

Jus' Sharn' a Tidbit – #27
—A TIME TO CELEBRATE IN THE MONTH OF DECEMBER (LIFE)—

(Part II)

Jus' Sharn' continues this week of celebrating Christ! Allow yourself to not only celebrate that you are still here, but most of all, to celebrate and commemorate the birth of our Lord and Savior Jesus Christ. Also known as the Redeemer and the Messiah, He was born for a purpose for us. So, let us celebrate this special event. If you can, look around you and see with a spiritual eye and worship Him.

> *"For unto us a child is born, unto us a son is given, and the government shall be upon his shoulder: and His name shall be called Wonderful, Counsellor, Mighty God,*

> *Everlasting Father, Prince of Peace."* **Isaiah 9:6 (NKJV)**

Unto us a child is born, this is our gift.

The government shall be upon His shoulders–like when Christ walked this earth, He carried our burdens–and carries them today through, grief, illnesses, pandemic, cancer, homelessness, stress, depression, suicidal thoughts, and more.

He is a wonderful Counsellor for our burdens. He is a mighty God and the everlasting Father. He will not forsake you for He is the Prince of Peace. He will give comfort, joy, peace, and strength.

> *"A time to weep, and a time to laugh; a time to mourn, and a time to dance."* **Ecclesiastes 3:4 (NKJV)**

Celebrate you and your family. Be encouraged. Peace and blessings.

Song of the Day: "Holy, Holy, Holy" by Donnie McClurkin

Jus' Sharn' a Tidbit – #28
—A TIME TO CELEBRATE IN THE MONTH OF DECEMBER (LIFE)—

(Part III)

Jus' Sharn' continues this week of celebrating Christ! Have you ever thought about the birth of Jesus Christ and why we should celebrate this joyous occasion? Why? Because we benefited from His birth. We all know the story of Christ's birth in a manger wrapped in swaddling cloth. A precious sacrificial gift of love to come into this world.

> *"Let the Redeemed of the Lord say so. Whom He has redeemed from the hand of the enemy."*
> **Psalm 107:2 (NKJV)**

He is the Redeemer. He paid for our sins. So, let us celebrate His birth with thanksgiving, love, and gladness.

Jesus is the light of this world and a gift from God. Appreciate life, keep Jesus within, and among you, do not exclude but include Him.

What a night to remember the birth of Jesus Christ! Hallelujah!

Sharing a few Scriptures with you to read. Let the words flow within your spirit.

> *"Therefore, the Lord himself will give you a sign: Behold, the virgin shall conceive and gear a Son, and shall call His name Immanuel."* **Isaiah 7:14 (NKJV)**

> *"And she will bring forth a Son, and you shall call His name Jesus, for He will save his people from their sins."* **Matthew 1:21 (NKJV)**

> *"So it was, that while they were there, the days were completed for her to be delivered. And she brought forth her firstborn, Son, and wrapped Him in swaddling cloths and laid Him in a manger, because there was no room for them in the inn."* **Luke 2:6-7 (NKJV)**

> *"And the Word became flesh and dwelt among us, and we beheld His glory, the glory as of*

> *the only begotten of the Father, full of grace and truth".* **John 1:14 (NKJV)**

Hallelujah! Thank you, Lord!

> *"Thanks be to God for His indescribable gift."*
> **2 Corinthians 9:15 (NKJV)**

Celebrate Christ, your family, and your friends.
God is in control.
Peace and blessings.

Song of the Day: "O Holy Night" by John P. Kee

Jus' Sharn' a Tidbit – #29
—Reflection of the Year 2020—

I pray all is well as you this last Jus' Sharn' tidbit of the year, and that you all had an enjoyable fulfilled Merry Christmas to celebrate the gift our all-loving God has given to the world. Now, let us reflect this week of our year of 2020: anxiety, stress, depression, suicidal thoughts, homelessness, losing of loved ones, COVID-19, presidential election, black lives matter… all lives matter to God.

This is New Year week countdown. Think and reflect as God does. He places the past into the sea of forgetfulness, but do you? Just think as you have been reading these tidbits and your spirit has been fed, are you willing to take the step of shedding the old skin for a renewal of you, your mind, your soul, and your spirit? Step into believing of the Word of God. Step into faith, joy, and peace of renewal, rebuilding, and restoration. It all waits for you.

> *"For I know the thoughts that I think toward you, says the Lord, thoughts of peace and not of evil, to give you a future and a hope."* **Jeremiah 29v11 (NKJV)**

> *"Brethren, I do not count myself yet to have apprehended, but one thing, I do: forgetting those things which are behind and reaching forward to those things which are ahead, I press toward the goal for the prize of the upward call of God in Christ Jesus."* **Philippians 3:13-14 (NKJV)**

> *"You crown the year with Your goodness and Your paths drip with abundance."* **Psalm 65:11 (NKJV)**

Jus' Sharn' wishes you a Happy New Year and many blessings and hopefully a new journey for the year of 2021! God is love and He loves each one of us.

Be encouraged.

Song of the Day: "Never Lost" by CeCe Winans

—CONCLUSION—

CONCLUSION: Even though we all have endured trials and tribulations, we made it through the calamities whether personal or within this world that we have witness. The word of God keeps us through our grief with comfort, our scars with His healing of compassion, love, and peace. I encourage you to keep this verse hidden in your heart.

> ***Psalm 121v1-(NKJV)**- I will life up my eyes to the hills from whence comes my help? My help comes from the Lord, who made heaven and earth.*

This is just a steppingstone in the right direction of what God wants from us, keep moving forward. Build the relationship with Him. ***Stay tuned for Volume II of Jus' Sharn"Tidbits...***

Peace & Blessings...

Jus' Sharn'

JUST ME...

My reasons for choosing butterflies as a signature symbol for Jus' Sharn', a butterfly represents diversity, freedom, transformation, a change within your inner and outer self, it represents beauty we go through a growing pain process from a cocoon being birth from darkness to light as we decide to follow Christ. When God created the earth He created a beauty, He filled the earth with colors and shapes. So, why are we boxing the earth in just black and white?

BIOGRAPHY

Silence can fill a room.

This statement makes you wonder, what does that mean? I am originally from the South, my upbringing raised in a Christian home by two parents, I was always told, you are too quiet, you are strange and weird, little did anyone knew I was listening and watching in silence. Is being silent a weapon? Being silent was looked upon me of being misjudged, misunderstood, and being rejected, but God turned it for good. Your presence and your silence are how God may use you.

What a journey a long time coming with this, this has been a self-confidence builder and for me to understand and receive who God says, "I am". Thank you, my Heavenly Father.

Jus' Sharn' Tidbit devotional book is filled with encouraging reminders of love, walking in faith, healing, hope, forgiveness, walk into your purpose. I can testify writing these "Tidbits" strengthened my relationship and walk with God, believe, and enjoy it will ease the daily stresses of life.

Printed in the USA
CPSIA information can be obtained
at www.ICGtesting.com
CBHW021909091224
18710CB00003B/24